THE WEATHER AND US

WEATHER REPORT

Ann and Jim Merk

The Rourke Corporation, Inc.
Vero Beach, Florida 32964

PHOTO CREDITS
© Lynn M. Stone: all photos except page 7 © Wyman Meinzer
page 21 © James P. Rowan and page 18 © Werner
Zehnder/Zegrahm Expeditions

Library of Congress Cataloging-in-Publication Data

Merk, Ann, 1952–
    The weather and us / by Ann and Jim Merk.
        p. cm. — (Weather report)
    Includes index
    ISBN 0-86593-387-1
    1. Weather—Juvenile literature. 2. Climatology—Juvenile
literature. [1. Weather 2. Climatology.]
I. Merk, Jim, 1952- . II. Title   III. Series: Merk, Ann, 1952- Weather
report.
QC981.3.M54 1994
551.5—dc20   94-13322
                                                      CIP
Printed in the USA   AC

TABLE OF CONTENTS

THE WEATHER AND US

Weather is what it is like outside on any day at any time. Weather is important to everyone. Weather has much to do with how we dress, how we build our homes and what we do outdoors. Weather sometimes has much to do with how we feel.

We can—and do—talk about the weather, but we can't change it. Weather changes by itself. In fact, weather is always changing. It changes with the time of day and the time of year.

Weather can make a field trip fun—or miserable!

CHANGING WEATHER

Weather changes as different kinds of air masses meet. An air mass is a large "pillow" of air. It might be warm or cold air, wet air or dry air.

When two air masses meet, they cause a change in weather conditions. A **front** forms where these two air masses meet. The front often brings rain or snow.

When two different air masses collide, rain or snow is likely

WHAT CAUSES WEATHER

Several things contribute to making the outdoor conditions we call weather.

One is the amount of sunshine that a place receives. Another is the **altitude**, or height, of a location above sea level. The higher the location, the cooler its air.

The nearness of mountains or large bodies of water have an impact on weather. The direction and amount of wind also affect weather.

Mountains and large bodies of water
have a direct impact on weather

CLIMATE

The weather that a place has over a long period of time is its **climate**. The desert, for example, may have a rainy day now and then, but the desert has a dry climate. One day's weather conditions do not always give us a good picture of an area's climate.

The same things that cause weather conditions create climate for an area. Oceans are one of the things that affect weather. Oceans give seaside locations a warmer, moister climate than places inland.

Low, wet clouds from the Pacific Ocean help keep Oregon's seaside climate mild and its forests green

Florida's warm, sunny climate has made it one of the nation's fastest growing states

Death Valley in the Mojave Desert, where the temperature once reached 134 degrees (Fahrenheit)

THE ATMOSPHERE

All weather occurs in the Earth's blanket of air, or **atmosphere**.

The atmosphere is made up of several layers. The air closest to the Earth's surface is what we breathe.

As a person, or plane, climbs upward, the air becomes "thinner." It contains less oxygen and makes breathing more difficult.

Jet airplanes fly in an upper level of air called the **stratosphere**. Passengers breathe easily only because systems in the airplane make the air breathable.

Jet airplanes fly in the stratosphere, high above mountain peaks

WIND

Wind is the movement of air. We can't see wind. We can feel wind, though, and see the movement of objects it blows.

Wind conditions are part of our weather. A blowing wind makes the air feel cooler than it really is.

Hard winds and windstorms, such as tornadoes and hurricanes, can cause major damage.

Differences in the temperatures of air masses cause wind. The speed of the wind several hundred feet above the Earth may be much different than the wind speed below.

Wind ruffles a bald eagle's head feathers as snowflakes fly

PLACES HOT AND COLD

The coldest places on Earth are near the north and south poles. Almost no one lives near the poles.

The poles are at the "ends" of the Earth. Some of the world's hottest places are near the **equator**. The equator is an imaginary line around the Earth's middle.

The Sahara Desert in North Africa once had a temperature of 136 degrees (Fahrenheit). That is 264 degrees warmer than Antarctica's record low of 128 degrees (Fahrenheit) below zero.

PLACES WET AND DRY

People live in the world's wettest and driest places, but not usually in large numbers.

Rain forests near the equator are the wettest places on land. Some "bathe" in more than an average of one inch of rain per day. Cloudy wet weather along the northwestern coast of North America has created pockets of rain forest in Washington, British Columbia and Southeast Alaska.

Deserts are dry places. They receive fewer than 10 inches of rain each year.

Warm, drizzly rain forests are the wettest places on the Earth's land surface

THE CLIMATE AND US

Not everyone agrees on what kind of climate is comfortable. But most people avoid extreme climates. Prospect Creek Camp in Alaska once had a low of 80 degrees below zero (Fahrenheit). Death Valley, California, is at the other extreme. It once had a temperature of 134 degrees (Fahrenheit).

Most people avoid mountain peaks, too, where weather can be savage. Mount Washington, New Hampshire, recorded a wind of 231 miles per hour!

Glossary

altitude (AL tuh tood) — the height of something above ground

atmosphere (AT muss feer) — the "blanket" of air around the Earth

climate (KLI mit) — the type of weather conditions that any place has over a long period of time

equator (ee KWAY ter) — the imaginary line drawn on maps around Earth's middle at equal distances from the north and south poles

front (FRONT) — the boundary between two different air masses

stratosphere (STRAH tuss feer) — an upper level of the atmosphere, about seven miles high

weather (WEH ther) — what it is like outside on any day at any time

INDEX

551.5   Merk, Ann, 1952-
Mer
        The weather and us

Anderson Elementary